SILK DESIGNS
OF THE
EIGHTEENTH
CENTURY

SILK DESIGNS OF THE EIGHTEENTH CENTURY

From the Victoria and Albert Museum, London

Edited with an Introduction

by Clare Browne

With 263 illustrations, 259 in color

THAMES AND HUDSON

Mr. Ogier. Octobr 12. 1748. for five

CONTENTS

Introduction

7

The Plates

9

The Formation of the Collection

105

The Designers

106

Bibliography

108

Index of Colour Plates

110

Silk design by
Anna Maria Garthwaite.
c. 1740 (5971.30).

Design for a silk damask
by Anna Maria Garthwaite.
dated 1743 (T.391–1971 p. 55).

Introduction

The English silk industry had its origins in the production of ribbons and half silks woven in London from the 16th century. The enormous growth in the weaving of pure silks came in the second half of the 17th century, with the market helped by returning stability at the end of the Civil Wars and demand for consumer goods in the American Colonies. The Huguenot contribution to the industry was extensive, not so much in numbers as in the successful application of textile skills and business acumen. Huguenots had begun to arrive in England in the late 16th century as refugees, and there were increasing migrations throughout the 17th century. They were among large numbers, from within England as well as abroad, attracted to the capital, and by 1700 the London silk industry had spread out from the City to Spitalfields.

During the 17th century the European market for fashionable dress silks had been dominated by material from France, especially Lyon. This was the competition for Spitalfields silks, which the industry expanded to meet. Production was stimulated by constant innovation in fashionable design, and a considerable export market. Between the 1680s and the 1770s there was almost continuous progress in the industry, aided by legislation that included the prohibition of printed calicoes in 1721; the prohibition of imported French silks in 1766; and, in 1773, the first of a series of Spitalfields Acts agreeing rates of pay, and so securing several decades of industrial peace. In the later 18th century the industry suffered financially from the fashion for smaller patterns and lighter fabrics, although reasonable stability was maintained until 1824, when Free Trade reform brought the repeal of the Act of 1766 and of the Spitalfields Acts. Effective from 1826, the legislation had immediate and crippling results, with French silks flooding the market and the collapse of the English industry.

The Development of Style

Although it came to develop its own individual character, woven silk design in England always had to compete with changes in fashion and technical advances in France in order to earn a share of the market.

The late 17th and first years of the 18th century had seen a fashion for extreme and unnatural patterns in silks. The earliest dated English designs, made by James Leman in 1706–07, still show some characteristics of this, with elongated patterns, motifs both strange and familiar and of different scale juxtaposed, and elements of chinoiserie and japonaiserie. Their strong reds and yellows are colour codes for different types of metal thread. From the early 1710s, Leman's increasingly sophisticated work shows the more bizarre motifs retreating while the designs retain their strong sense of movement, and their various elements form interconnecting layers of increasing elaboration.

As the decade progressed, this tendency became more pronounced. The richer silks were luxuriant, with their semi-naturalistic flowers entwined around gold scrolls on grounds of silver or gold. Lighter-weight silks had delicate floral sprigs, sometimes asymmetrical, sometimes enclosed between vertical stripes. Out of these fashions, by 1720 a particular style had developed which came to dominate silk design for the next twelve years. It comprised a more or less elaborate framework with a point (mirror) repeat, which gave an air of formality even to very light and delicate patterns. The most characteristic designs from these years had a lace-like pattern in the ground, or heavily diapered scrolls, interwoven with leaves and flowers which grew larger and more naturalistic towards the end of the 1720s.

In 1732 a revolution in silk design in France brought totally new inspiration, as designers turned away from surface texture to the depiction of three-dimensional form. One designer in particular, Jean Revel, introduced a method of shading, called *points rentrés*, whereby tones of colour were dovetailed in weaving, to extraordinary effect. To show this to advantage, designs grew larger, until they reached a massive scale in the years 1740–42. Colours were bold and there were large areas of plain silk to set off the designs. The English designer Anna Maria Garthwaite possessed a number of French designs from the 1730s in her own collection, and the influence on her work of this new development in style is immediately apparent, including the typical motif of the tree upon an island, hung with enormous flowers.

By 1742 these design elements were being drawn to half scale or in a lighter style, the forerunners of a totally new naturalism. The silks designed and woven in Spitalfields in the 1740s achieved a particularly English interpretation of Rococo, with an accurate rendering of botanical detail, flowers scattered across an open ground, usually in an asymmetrical arrangement, and clear, true colours. This style continued through the 1740s, the clarity of the designs giving way to more elaborate patterned grounds towards the end of the decade.

The return of French influence is apparent in English silk design of the 1750s and 1760s. Flowers became stylized and typically might be combined with meandering trails of simulated fur, feathers, ribbons or lace for *trompe-l'oeil* effect; warp-printing (producing *chiné* or 'clouded' silks) was increasingly popular; and there was a great variety of weaves and types of silk and metal thread to set off the patterns. These stiff, heavily patterned silks were suitable for fashions of the 1760s, but had subsequently to adapt for an increasingly informal style of dressing.

From 1770 motifs reduced further and further in scale, frequently combining with broad and narrow stripes. The taste for Neo-Classical style was met with tiny wreaths, rosettes or ovals with formal sprigs; colours in the 1770s were predominantly pastels. By the 1780s patterns were becoming increasingly abstract. Stripes in dark colours dominate the pattern books for some years, but they had disappeared by 1795, and the last years of the 18th century and the early 19th saw little variation in the taste for small and subtle repeating patterns, given variety with metal threads or gauze weaves. The collapse of the industry in 1826 came before the recently introduced Jacquard loom was given the chance to show its capacity for elaborate, textured and large-patterned silks.

1 Silk design by James Leman,
dated 1706/7.

2 Silk design by James Leman
for a flowered satin dated 1706/7.
It had two pattern wefts, 'one to
continue ye other to change'.
3 Silk design by James Leman
for a 'Flow[d]: Sattin with changeing
& Brocade', dated 1707.

5

4 Silk design by James Leman,
dated 1706/7.
5 Silk design by James Leman,
dated 1708.

6 Silk design by Christopher Baudouin, dated 1707.
7 Silk design by James Leman, dated 1708.
8 Chasuble, the silks French, *c.* 1707–8. These can be dated by comparison with designs by James Leman from 1707 (pls 1, 3) and from 1708 (pl.9).

9

11

10

9   Silk design by James Leman, dated 1708.
10   Silk design by James Leman, dated 1708/9.
11   Silk design by James Leman, dated 1709.
12   Silk design by James Leman, dated 1709.
13   Silk design by James Leman, dated 1709.

12

13

14

15

16

14 Silk design by James Leman, dated 1710.
15 Silk design by James Leman, dated 1710.
16 Silk design by James Leman, dated 1710.
17 Silk design by James Leman, dated 1710.

18

19

20

21

22

18 Silk design by James Leman, dated 1711.
19 Silk design by James Leman, dated 1711.
20 Silk design by James Leman, dated 1711.
21 Silk design by James Leman, dated 1710/11.
22 and **23** *(detail)* Silk design, almost certainly by James Leman, dated 1711.

24

25

24 Silk design by James Leman,
dated 1711.
25 Silk design by James Leman
for a brocaded damask, dated 1711.
26 Silk design by James Leman,
dated 1711, 'taken from a Dutch stuff'.

26

27 Silk design by James Leman, dated 1711/12.
28 Silk design by James Leman, dated 1713.

29

29 Silk design, almost certainly
by James Leman, *c.* 1717.
30 Silk design by James Leman,
dated 1716.
31 Silk design by James Leman,
dated 1717.

30

31

32

33

32 Silk design by Joseph Dandridge, dated 1718.
33 Silk design by Joseph Dandridge, dated 1718.
34 Silk design by Christopher Baudouin, dated 1718.

34

35

38

36

37

35 Silk design probably by
James Leman, dated 1719:20.
36 Silk design by James Leman,
dated 1719:20.
37 One of Anna Maria Garthwaite's
'Patterns not my own', *c*. 1720.
38 and **39** *(detail)* Silk design
by Joseph Dandridge, dated 1720.

40

41

42

40 Silk design, almost certainly by
Christopher Baudouin, dated 1723/4.
41 Silk design by James Leman, dated 1721.
42 Silk design by Anna Maria Garthwaite,
c. 1726.
43 Silk design by Anna Maria Garthwaite,
before 1730.

43

44

45

46

44 Design by Anna Maria Garthwaite,
before 1730.
45 Silk design by Anna Maria Garthwaite,
c. 1730.
46 Silk design by Anna Maria Garthwaite,
c. 1726–7.

47

48

47 Silk design by Anna Maria
Garthwaite, *c.* 1726.
48 Silk design by Anna Maria
Garthwaite, before 1730.
49 Silk design by Anna Maria
Garthwaite, dated 1729.
50 Silk design by Anna Maria
Garthwaite, *c.* 1730.
51 Silk design by Anna Maria
Garthwaite, before 1730.
52 Silk design by Anna Maria
Garthwaite, dated '1731 & 32'.
53 Silk design by Anna Maria
Garthwaite, *c.* 1732.
54 Silk design by
Anna Maria Garthwaite, *c.* 1732.

49

50

51

52   53   54

55

56

55 *(detail)* and **56** Silk design
by Anna Maria Garthwaite, *c.* 1730.

57

57 Double tabby silk
woven from or after a design by
Anna Maria Garthwaite (pl.60).

58

60

58 Silk design by
Anna Maria Garthwaite,
dated 1733.
59 Silk design by
Anna Maria Garthwaite,
c. 1733.
60 Silk design by
Anna Maria Garthwaite,
dated 1733.
61 Silk design by
Anna Maria Garthwaite,
c. 1733.
62 and **63** *(detail)* Silk design,
possibly a copy by
Anna Maria Garthwaite
of a French original,
dated 1733.

59

61

62

64

65

67

66

64 Silk design by
Anna Maria Garthwaite, dated 1733.
65 Silk design by
Anna Maria Garthwaite, c. 1733.
66 Silk design, French,
probably by Jean Revel, dated 1735.
67 Silk design by
Anna Maria Garthwaite, dated 1735.

68

68 Silk design, possibly
by Joseph Dandridge, *c.* 1734.

69

70

71

69   Silk design by Anna Maria Garthwaite, dated 1735.
70   Silk designs by Anna Maria Garthwaite, dated 1736.
71   Silk design by Anna Maria Garthwaite, dated 1738.

72

72 Silk design by Anna Maria Garthwaite, dated 1738.

73 Silk design possibly by
the Lyon designer Courtois,
or an English copy,
dated 1733.
74 Silk design, possibly by
Courtois. *c.* 1733–34.
75 Silk design, French,
possibly after a design by Courtois,
dated 1733.
76 Silk design by
Anna Maria Garthwaite. *c.* 1733.
77 Silk design, French,
dated 1733 or 1734.

74

73

76

75

77

78

79

78 Silk design by
Anna Maria Garthwaite, *c.* 1735.
79 Design for a waistcoat by
Anna Maria Garthwaite, *c.* 1735.
80 Silk design, French,
dated 1733 (?).
81 Silk design, probably French,
c. 1733/4.
82 Silk design, French,
c. 1734-35.
83 Silk design by
Anna Maria Garthwaite, *c.* 1734.
84 Silk design, French,
dated 1734.
85 Silk design, French,
mid-1730s.

80

81

82

83

84

85

86

88

90

87

89

91

86 Silk design, French, dated 1739.
87 Silk design, French, dated 1739.
88 Silk design, French, dated 1739.
89 Silk design, French, dated 1739.
90 Silk design, French, 1739.
91 and **92** *(detail)* Silk design,
French, dated 1739.

93

94

96

95

93 Design, possibly for an embroidered skirt or waistcoat border, French, dated 1739.
94 Silk design, French, dated 1739.
95 Silk design, French, dated 1739.
96 Design for a tobine (warp-patterned silk) by Anna Maria Garthwaite, 1741.
97 Design for a tobine (warp-patterned silk) by Anna Maria Garthwaite, 1741.

97

98

99

98 Silk design by Anna Maria Garthwaite, 1741.
99 Silk design by Anna Maria Garthwaite, dated 1740.
100 Silk design by Anna Maria Garthwaite, 1741.
101 Silk design by Anna Maria Garthwaite, 1741.
102 Silk design by Anna Maria Garthwaite, dated 1740.

100

101

102

103

104

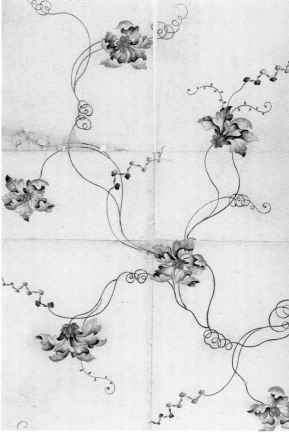

105

103 Silk design by Anna
Maria Garthwaite, dated 1739.
104 Silk design by Anna
Maria Garthwaite, *c.* 1740.
105 Silk design by Anna
Maria Garthwaite, 1741.
106 Silk design by Anna
Maria Garthwaite, *c.* 1740.

The White in the Flowers
the Brocade

107

108

107 and **108** *(detail)*   Silk design by Anna Maria Garthwaite, 1742.

Mr Nauteir. May 10 1742

109

110

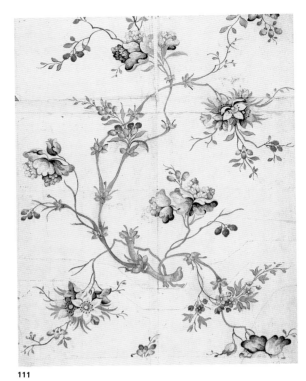

111

Mr Gregory. March. 31. 1742. a Brocade Tissue 5 Shillis

112

113

109 Silk design by Anna
Maria Garthwaite, dated 1742.
110 Silk design by Anna
Maria Garthwaite, 1742.
111 Silk design by Anna
Maria Garthwaite, 1741.
112 Silk design by Anna
Maria Garthwaite, dated 1742.
113 Silk designs by Anna
Maria Garthwaite, dated 1741/2.
114 Silk design by
Anna Maria Garthwaite, 1742.

114

Capt. Lekeux, Dropt. Sept 20. 1742

115

115 Silk design by
Anna Maria Garthwaite,
dated 1742.
116 Silk design by
Anna Maria Garthwaite, 1742.

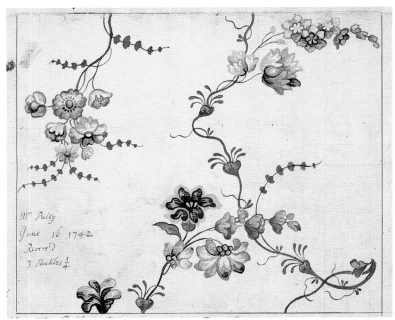

117

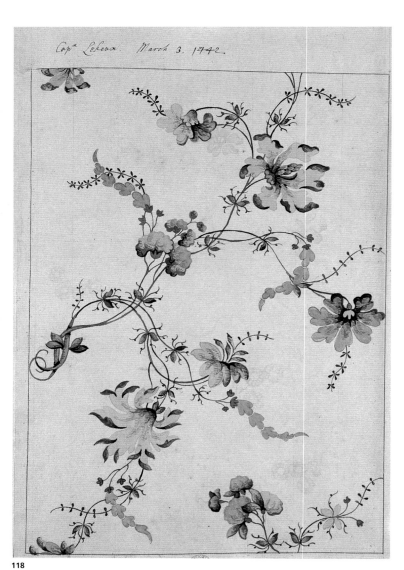

118

119

58

Cap.ⁿ Baker. July 9. 1742. 2 Shuttles. ½ y.ᵈ

120

117 Silk design by
Anna Maria Garthwaite, dated 1742.
118 Silk design by
Anna Maria Garthwaite, dated 1742.
119 Silk design by
Anna Maria Garthwaite, dated 1742.
120 *(with background picture detail)*
Silk design by
Anna Maria Garthwaite, dated 1742.

121, 122 *(details)* and **123**
Silk design by Anna Maria Garthwaite, 1742.
124 *(detail)* and **126**
Silk design by Anna Maria Garthwaite, dated 1742.
125 Silk designs by Anna Maria Garthwaite, dated 1742.
127 Silk design by Anna Maria Garthwaite, dated 1742.

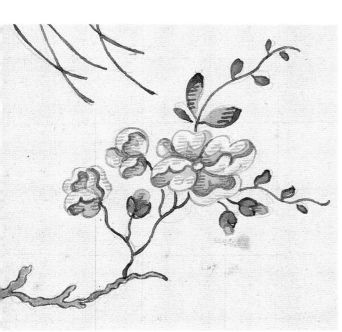

Mr Ogeir. in the Square. Nov.r 3. 1742. 3 shuttles Bro.

124 **126**

Mr Ogeir. July 8 1742. Tiered Patts.

Mr Gobbee Mr Carr. June 22. 1742. Revers'd

Cap.t Baker June 24 1742. Point & Com. 4 shuttles ½

125 **127**

128 and **129** *(detail)*
Silk design by
Anna Maria Garthwaite,
dated 1742.

129

130

131

130 Silk design by
Anna Maria Garthwaite, dated 1743.
131 Silk design by
Anna Maria Garthwaite, dated 1743.

132

133

132 Silk design by Anna Maria Garthwaite, dated 1743.

133 Silk design by Anna Maria Garthwaite for a 'Tobine Lut[estring] Heartsease', dated 1743.

134 Silk design by Anna Maria Garthwaite, dated 1743.

135 Silk design by Anna Maria Garthwaite, dated 1743.

136

138

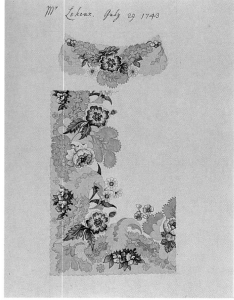

137

136 Silk design by Anna Maria
Garthwaite, dated 1743.
137 'A silver and silk shape for
a waistcoat', design by Anna
Maria Garthwaite, dated 1743.
138 Silk design by Anna Maria
Garthwaite, dated 1743.
139 Silk design by Anna Maria
Garthwaite, dated 1743.
140 and **141** *(detail)* 'A silver
shape for a coat', design by Anna
Maria Garthwaite, dated 1743.

Mr Gregory. Octob. 14. 1743

111¼

139

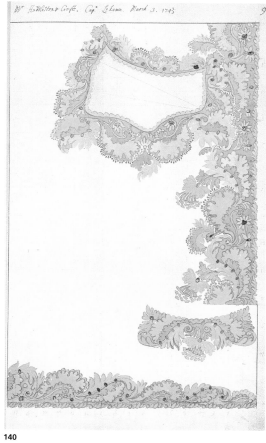

Mr Huddleston & Croft. Capt Lekeux. March 3. 1743

9

140

141

Mr Vauteir. July 6. 1743.

142

144

Mr Carr. Mr Mason. Octobr 19. 1743.

143   145

146

142 and **144** *(detail)*
Silk design by
Anna Maria Garthwaite,
dated 1743.
143 *(detail)* and **145**
Silk design by
Anna Maria Garthwaite,
dated 1743.
146 Silk design by
Anna Maria Garthwaite,
dated 1744.
147 Silk design by
Anna Maria Garthwaite,
dated 1744.
148 Silk design by
Anna Maria Garthwaite,
dated 1744.

147

148

149

149 Silk design by Anna Maria
Garthwaite. dated 1745.
150 Fragment of brocaded silk
woven from a silk design
by Anna Maria Garthwaite,
dated 1745 (pl.151).
151 Silk design by Anna Maria
Garthwaite. dated 1745.
152 Silk design by Anna Maria
Garthwaite. dated 1745.
153 'A Silver Shap'd Wastcote'.
design by Anna Maria Garthwaite,
dated 1745.
154 Silk design by Anna Maria
Garthwaite. dated 1745.

150

Mr Palmer. Mr Vautier April 3. 1745

151

Mr Leleux. October 12. 1745

153

Mr Gregory March 23 1745

152

Mr Leleux Nov. 6. 1745

154

156

155 'A Silver & Silk Wastcoat', design
by Anna Maria Garthwaite, dated 1747.
156 Silk design by
Anna Maria Garthwaite, dated 1748.
157 Silk design by
Anna Maria Garthwaite, dated 1747.
158 Silk designs by
Anna Maria Garthwaite, dated 1747.
159 Silk design by
Anna Maria Garthwaite, dated 1747.
160 Silk designs by
Anna Maria Garthwaite, dated 1747.
161 Silk designs by
Anna Maria Garthwaite, dated 1748.

155

157

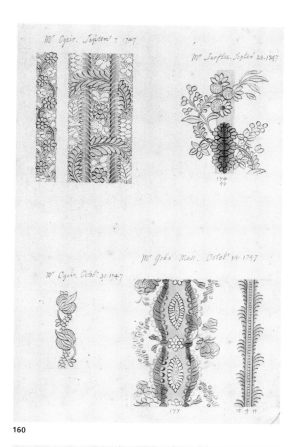

160

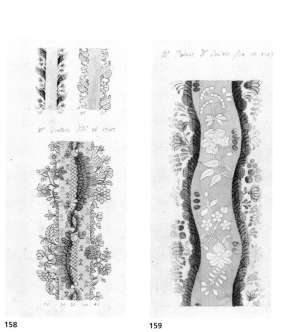

158

159

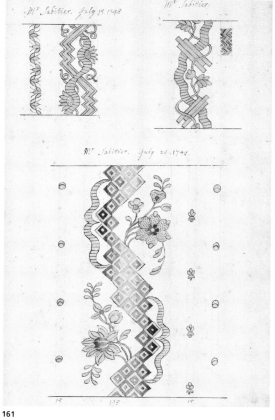

161

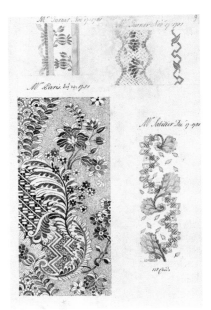

162

164

163

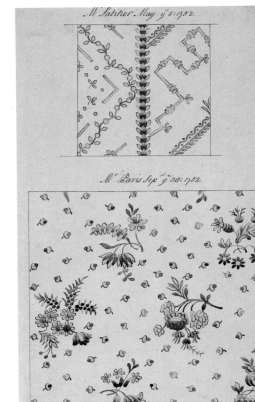

165

162 Silk design by
Anna Maria Garthwaite,
dated 1750.
163 Silk design by
Anna Maria Garthwaite,
dated 1752.
164 Silk design by
Anna Maria Garthwaite,
dated 1751.
165 Silk designs by
Anna Maria Garthwaite,
dated 1752.

166

167

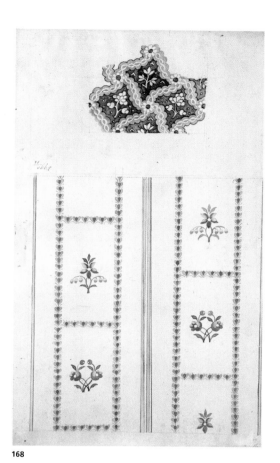

168

166 Silk designs by
Anna Maria Garthwaite,
dated 1753.
167 Silk designs by
Anna Maria Garthwaite,
dated 1752 or 1754.
168 Silk designs by
Anna Maria Garthwaite,
dated 1754 and 1755.

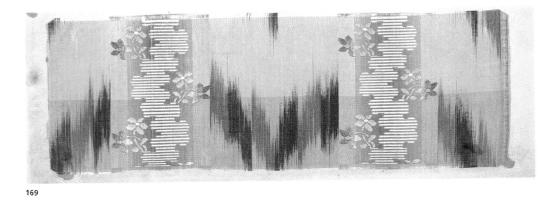

169

170

171

169 Sample of tobine
from pattern book of
Batchelor, Ham and Perigal,
late 1750s.

170 Sample from pattern book
of Batchelor, Ham and Perigal,
c. 1760.

171 Samples from pattern book
of Batchelor, Ham and Perigal,
1750s.

172 Sample from pattern book
of Batchelor, Ham and Perigal,
c. 1760 (?) or, *c.* 1767 (?).

173 Sample from order book
of unknown French merchant,
early 1760s.

174 Sample from order book
of unknown French merchant,
early 1760s.

175 Samples from pattern
book of Batchelor, Ham and
Perigal, early 1760s.

172

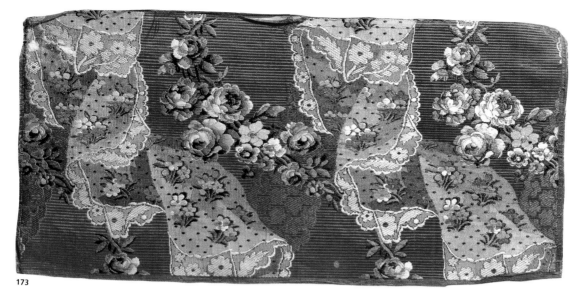

173

174

175

176

177

178

179

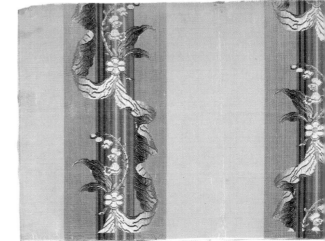

180

181

176 Samples from pattern book of Batchelor, Ham and Perigal, early 1760s.
177 Samples from pattern book of Batchelor, Ham and Perigal, early 1760s.
178 Samples of *chiné* (warp-printed) silks from order book of unknown French merchant, early 1760s.
179 English silk dated 1764 from order book of unknown French merchant.
180 and **181** *(detail)* Sample from pattern book of Batchelor, Ham and Perigal, *c.* 1760.

182

182 Silk design, French, Lyon,
L. Galy Gallien, dated 1762.
183 Silk design, French, Lyon,
L. Galy Gallien & Cie, dated 1763.
184 Silk design, French, Lyon,
L. Galy Gallien, dated 1762 . . . 1763.
185 Silk design, French, Lyon,
c. 1760–65.
186 Silk design, French, Lyon,
Galy Gallien & Cie, dated 1762.
187 Silk design, French, Lyon,
L. Galy Gallien & Cie, dated 1771.
188 Silk design, French, Lyon,
L. Galy Gallien & Cie, dated 1762.
189 Silk design, French, Lyon,
L. Galy Gallien & Cie, dated 1771.

183

187

188

189

190   Samples from pattern book of
Batchelor, Ham and Perigal, dated 1775.
191   Samples from pattern book of
Batchelor, Ham and Perigal, dated 1778.
192   Samples from order book
of an unknown French merchant.
The French sample early 1760s with
English samples inserted later,
one dated 1776.
193   Sample from pattern book of
Batchelor, Ham and Perigal, dated 1776.

192

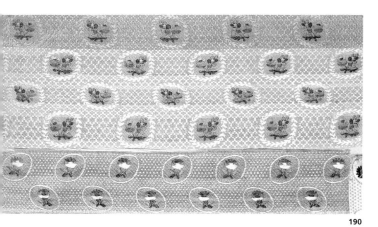

190

191

193

194 Sample from pattern book of
Batchelor, Ham and Perigal,
dated 1774.
195 Sample from pattern book of
Batchelor, Ham and Perigal,
dated 1775.
196 Sample from pattern book of
Batchelor, Ham and Perigal,
dated 1775.

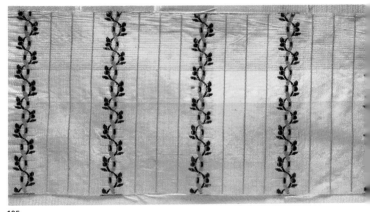

195

194

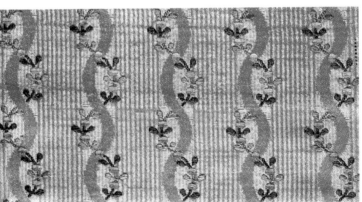

196

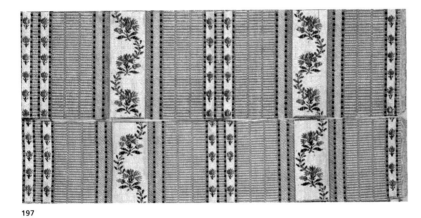

197

197 and **198** *(detail)* Samples from pattern book of Batchelor, Ham and Perigal, *c.* 1772–73.

198

199 and **200** *(detail)* Sample from pattern book of Batchelor, Ham and Perigal, *c.* 1772–73.

199

200

201

202

201 Samples from pattern book of Batchelor, Ham and Perigal, dated 1779.
202 Sample from pattern book of Batchelor, Ham and Perigal, dated 1782.
203 Sample from pattern book of Batchelor, Ham and Perigal, dated 1779.
204 Samples from pattern book of Batchelor, Ham and Perigal, dated 1782.
205 Sample of striped *chiné* from pattern book possibly of J & J Jourdain, *c.* 1784–85.
206 Samples from pattern book of Batchelor, Ham and Perigal, dated 1781.
207 Samples from pattern book of Batchelor, Ham and Perigal, dated 1784.
208 Undated samples from pattern book possibly of J & J Jourdain.

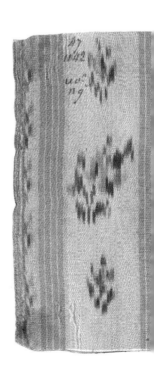

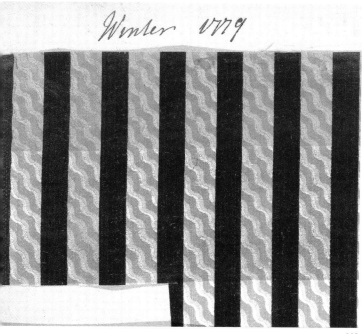

203

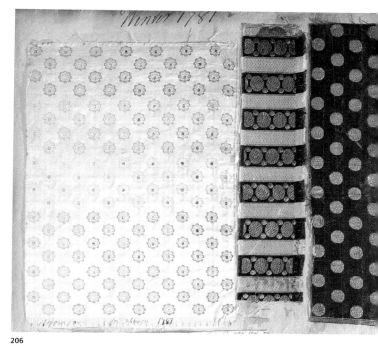

206

204

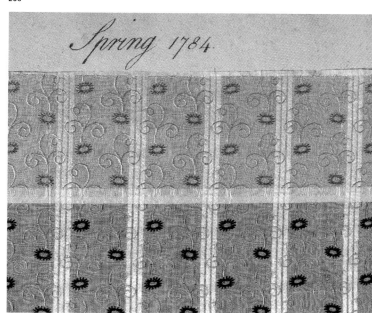

207

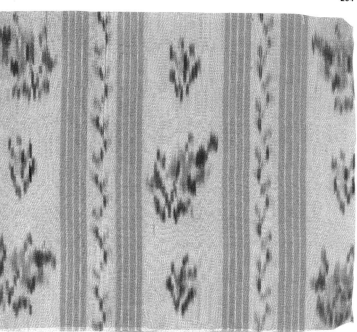

205

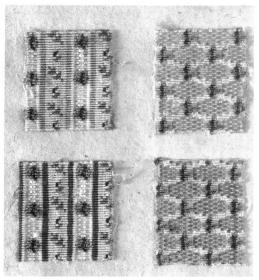

208

209

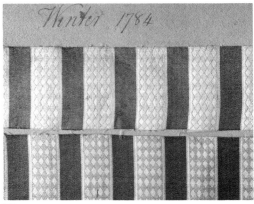

Winter 1784

210

Winter 1787

211

212

213

214

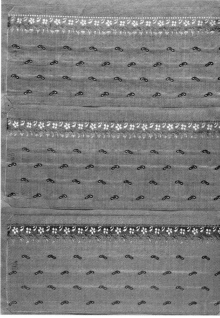

215

209 Samples from pattern book of Maze and Steer, 1787.

210 Samples from pattern book of Batchelor, Ham and Perigal, dated 1784.

211 Sample from pattern book of Batchelor, Ham and Perigal, dated 1787.

212 Samples from pattern book of Batchelor, Ham and Perigal, dated 1786.

213 Samples from pattern book of Batchelor, Ham and Perigal, dated 1789.

214 Samples from pattern book of Batchelor, Ham and Perigal, dated 1788.

215 Samples from pattern book of Maze and Steer, 1789.

216 Waistcoat woven by Maze and Steer in 1789 which can be identified from their pattern book (pl.215).

217

221

218

219

217 Samples from pattern book
of Maze and Steer, 1786.
218 Sample from pattern book
of Maze and Steer, 1786.
219 Sample from pattern book
of Maze and Steer, 1787.
220 Sample from pattern book
of Maze and Steer, 1788.
221 Sample from pattern book
of Maze and Steer, 1786.
222 Samples from pattern book
of Maze and Steer, 1787.
There is a waistcoat of this design
in the Museum of London.
223 Samples in silk and linen
from pattern book of
Maze and Steer, probably 1790.
There is a waistcoat of this design
in the Royal Albert Memorial
Museum, Exeter.
224 Samples from pattern book
of Maze and Steer, 1788.
There is a waistcoat of this design
in the V&A.
225 Samples from pattern book
of Maze and Steer, 1788.
There is a waistcoat of this design
in the Royal Albert Memorial
Museum, Exeter.
226 Waistcoat woven by
Maze and Steer, 1789,
which can be identified from
their pattern book (pl.227).
227 Samples from pattern book
of Maze and Steer, 1789.

220

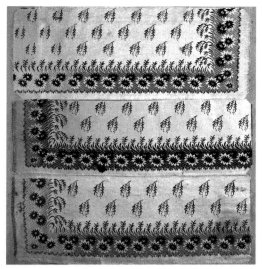

222

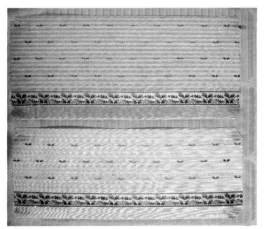

223

224

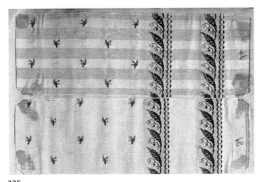

225

226

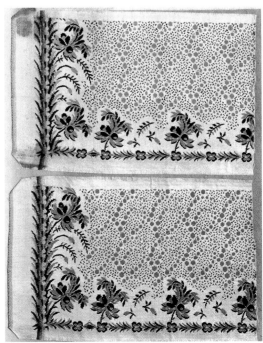

227

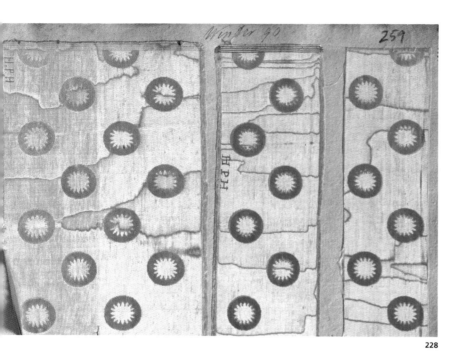

228

230

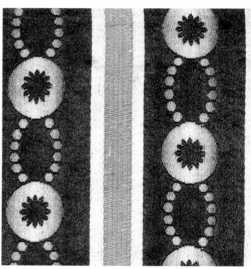

231

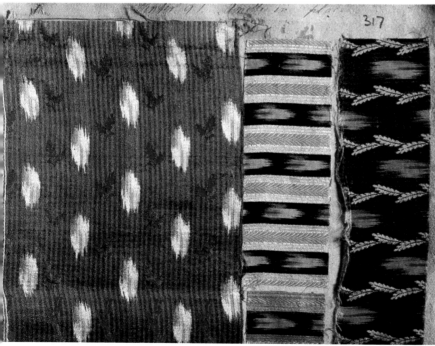

229

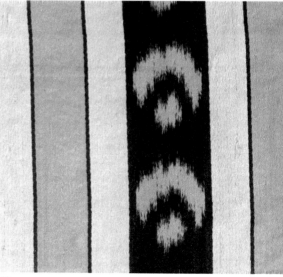

232

228 Samples from pattern book
of Harvey, Perigal and Ham,
successors to Batchelor, Ham and
Perigal, dated 1790.
229 Samples from pattern book
of Harvey, Perigal and Ham,
dated 1791.
230 Sample from pattern book
of Harvey, Ham and Perigal, 1790.
231 Sample from pattern book
of Harvey, Ham and Perigal, 1790.
232 Sample from pattern book
possibly of Harvey, Ham and
Perigal, c. 1792–94 (1793 onwards
Jourdain and John Ham).

233

234

235

233 Sample from pattern book
possibly of Harvey, Ham and Perigal,
c. 1792–94 (1793 onwards
Jourdain and John Ham).
234 Skirt flounce, sample from
pattern book of Harvey, Ham
and Perigal, 1792.
235 Skirt flounce, sample from
pattern book possibly of Harvey,
Ham and Perigal, *c.* 1792–94
(1793 onwards Jourdain and John Ham).

236

238

237

239

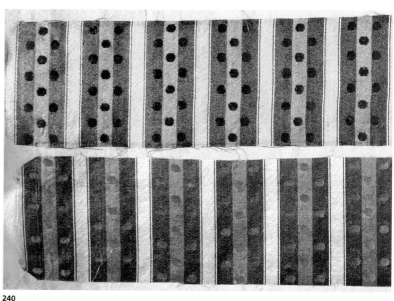

240

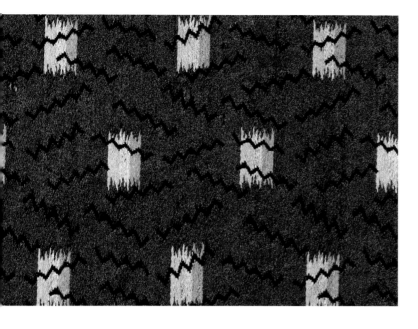

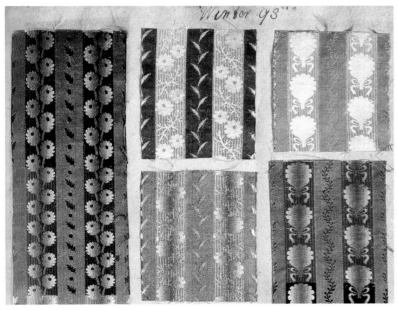

241

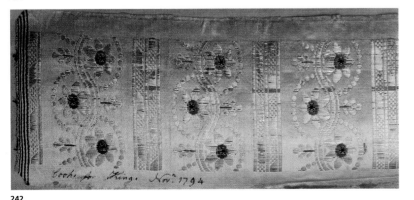

242

236 Samples from pattern book possibly of Harvey, Ham and Perigal, *c.* 1792–94 (1793 onwards Jourdain and John Ham).

237 Samples from pattern book of Jourdain and John Ham, successors to Harvey, Perigal and Ham, dated 1793. The change in partnership took place early in 1793.

238 Sample from pattern book possibly of Harvey, Ham and Perigal, *c.* 1792–94 (1793 onwards Jourdain and John Ham).

239 Sample from pattern book of Harvey, Perigal and Ham, whose initials appear in one corner, dated 1792.

240 Samples from pattern book possibly of Jourdain and John Ham, *c.* 1795–1802.

241 Samples from pattern book of Jourdain and John Ham, dated 1793.

242 Sample from pattern book of Jourdain and John Ham. dated 1794.

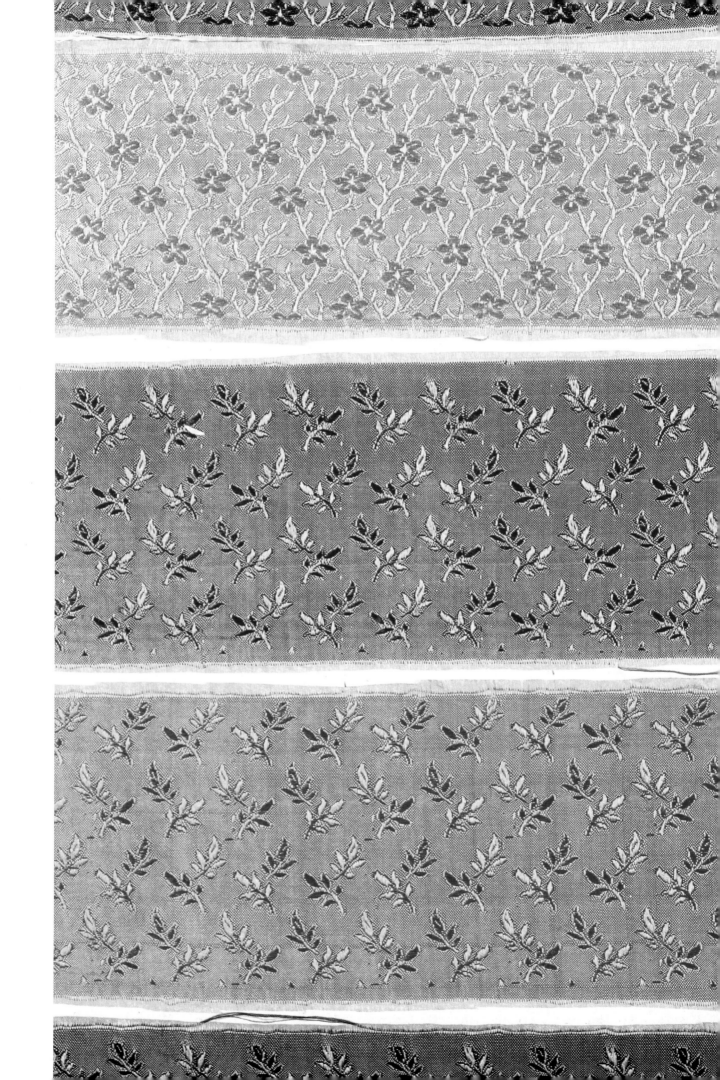

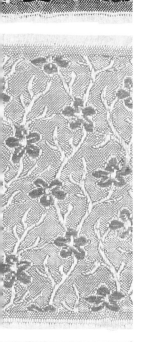

244

243 *(detail)* and 244 Samples from pattern book possibly of Jourdain and John Ham, *c.* 1795–1802.
245 Samples from pattern book possibly of Jourdain and John Ham, *c.* 1795–1802.
246 Samples from pattern book possibly of Jourdain and John Ham, *c.* 1795–1802.

245

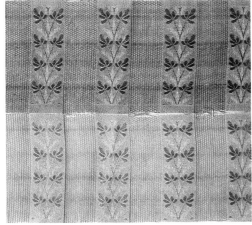

246

243

247 Sample from pattern book
of Jourdain and John Ham, dated 1801.
248 Samples from pattern book
of Jourdain and John Ham, dated 1805.
249 Sample from pattern book
of Jourdain and John Ham, dated 1804.
250 Samples from pattern book
of Jourdain and John Ham, dated 1805.

249

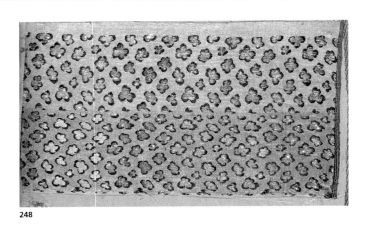

247

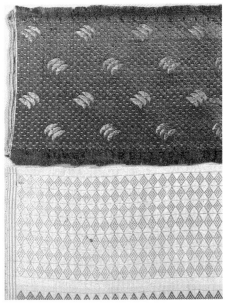

248

250

251

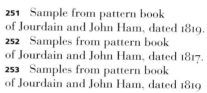

251 Sample from pattern book
of Jourdain and John Ham, dated 1819.
252 Samples from pattern book
of Jourdain and John Ham, dated 1817.
253 Samples from pattern book
of Jourdain and John Ham, dated 1819

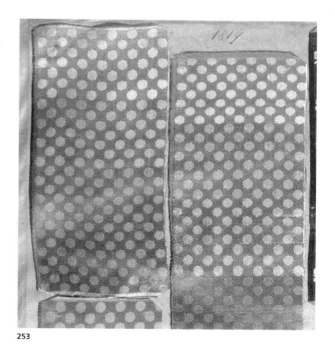

253

252

254

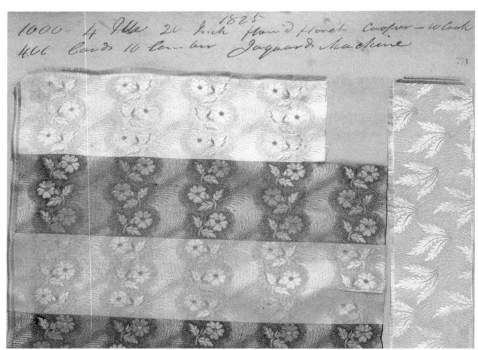

1000 — 4 Idle 20 high Plan'd Floret Cooper — black
400 Cards 10 lumber Jacquard Machine

1825

255

254 Page of samples from pattern book
of Jourdain and John Ham, with a sample
of fabric for Carlton House dated 1817.
255 and **256** *(detail)* Jacquard woven
sample from pattern book of Jourdain
and John Ham, dated 1825.

256

257

258

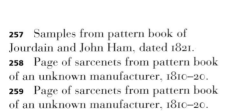

257 Samples from pattern book of
Jourdain and John Ham, dated 1821.
258 Page of sarcenets from pattern book
of an unknown manufacturer, 1810–20.
259 Page of sarcenets from pattern book
of an unknown manufacturer, 1810–20.

259

The Formation of the Collection

The 18th-century designs, woven silks and pattern books illustrated here have been acquired by the Victoria and Albert Museum over a period of more than one hundred years, and are part of a collection providing unparalleled coverage of the development of the English silk industry. The stylistic developments during the first half of the century unfold year by year, in some cases season by season, in the designs of James Leman and Anna Maria Garthwaite, along with the work by other designers they commissioned or collected. The later years of the century are illustrated with the series of dated pattern books from the Warner Archive.

In 1991 the museum acquired from Vanners Silks Ltd a group of ninety-seven silk designs, mostly by James Leman, which had been on loan for a number of years (museum numbers E.1861.1 to 106-1991). The designs, dating from 1706 to 1716, provide evidence of considerable sophistication in the early 18th-century English silk industry, and have led to the reattribution of a number of textiles previously presumed to be French or Italian. The designs by Leman himself, first as an apprentice, and later a manufacturer, would have been woven by the Leman journeymen in their own workshop or by independent journeymen weavers. They are mostly dated and contain much technical detail necessary to transfer them, via squared point-paper, to the loom.

A group of eighty designs, by Leman or collected by him, and ranging in date from 1717 to 1722, had been given to the museum in 1862 by a Mr G.W. Sheriff of Streatham (they were formally registered as part of the collection in 1909: museum numbers E.4440 to 4519-1909). The cover of the set was labelled 'Pattern Book of the Late Firm of Liddiard & Co. Circa 1718'. They include at least two designs almost certainly by Christopher Baudouin (fl.1680s– pre 1736), and eighteen by Joseph Dandridge (1665–1746).

The majority of Anna Maria Garthwaite's designs were acquired by the museum in 1868; there is no record of their provenance over the preceding century (museum numbers 5970 to 5990). This group range in date from the 1720s through to 1756, with just three gaps, one of these spectacularly filled by the acquisition in 1971 of three bound volumes, for the years 1743 and part of 1744, containing some of her most accomplished work (museum numbers T.391 to 393-1971). These had been found at a worsted spinning factory in Yorkshire, presumably acquired at some time in the past as a design source. Now only her work from 1746 and 1750 is completely missing, though it is not possible to say whether all of her early designs have been preserved. The designs are almost all dated, and annotated with the name of the weaver or mercer, sometimes both, who commissioned them. Among her own work, the designs collected by her include examples by other English and French designers.

Part of the archive of the textile firm of Warners was dispersed in 1972, and the museum was able to acquire a total of twenty-five pattern books, with other material, thirteen of them containing 18th- and early 19th-century woven silks (museum numbers T.373 to 385-1972). The Warner Archive had been built upon the archives of a succession of firms which Benjamin Warner took over in the late 19th century, and since they likewise had previously taken over other firms the archive dated back to the middle of the 18th century. The pattern books cover seven decades, from the mid-1750s until the repeal of the Spitalfields Acts in 1826 and the collapse of the English silk industry. They contain samples in many colourways, from which mercers could place their orders, and are often annotated with the name of the mercer, the date and the name of the journeyman weaver responsible for the work.

The museum also acquired from the Warner Archive a group of thirty-two French designs for woven silks, dating between 1761 and 1771, and mostly inscribed 'L. Galy Gallien' or 'L. Gallien & Cie'. They are stamped with the name Robert Ruepp, a French designer in the late 19th century, and were presumably part of the resources of his design studio; they were probably acquired by Warners in the 1920s.

The Designers

Anna Maria Garthwaite

Her family connections, her will and the evidence of the designs themselves make up virtually all that is known about Anna Maria Garthwaite. She was born on 14 March 1689/90, the daughter of the Reverend Ephraim Garthwaite of Grantham, Lincolnshire, and his wife Rejoyce. Her sister Mary was married to Robert Danny, Rector of Spofforth near York, and it seems likely that Anna Maria joined their household on the death of her father in 1719. Danny was previously Chaplain to the Chancellor of Cambridge University, and to the Duke of Somerset, and his sister-in-law would have enjoyed educated, intellectual company at Spofforth. With this background, there is no obvious explanation how or why she obtained the artistic and technical training that must have been necessary to equip her as a successful silk designer. By the time of Danny's death in 1729/30, she had already produced the series of designs inscribed 'In York, before I came to London' and was sending work down to the capital: 'this was sent to London with the Rul'd Paper before I came up'.

Garthwaite moved to London with her widowed sister Mary in 1730, and lived in Spitalfields until her death in 1763. She worked freelance, producing designs for both master weavers and mercers, as many as eighty a year. Her patterns before she arrived in London show her experimenting with different styles, and some may be intended for embroidery or lace, but the careful indication of a repeat on several of these early designs proves they were meant to be woven.

Once she had arrived in London she evidently understood very quickly the need to design for particular types of fabric, and her work is grouped, into 'Gold Stuffs', 'Brocades from 1735–40' or 'Damasks'. Part of her success must have lain in her understanding of the medium, and there is very little evidence in the designs of redrawing or adaptation. She knew the effects made by different weaves, and noted the number of shuttles, the colours for changes, the type of repeat and the number of cords required on many of her patterns. She also collected the work of other designers, including 'Patterns by Different Hands' and 'French Patterns' alongside her own designs. Her interest in natural form, and talent for depicting it, was most evident during the dominant fashion for botanical realism in the 1740s, but it characterized her designs throughout her working life.

James Leman

James Leman was born into a weaving family, of Huguenot descent. His father, Peter, had been admitted to the London Weavers' Company in 1674, and was described as 'natif de Cantorbury'; he may have been descended from the Leman family who are recorded as coming to Canterbury from Tourcoing to escape religious persecution in the late 16th century. James Leman was born c.1688, and apprenticed in 1702 to his father, the family by now living at Stewart Street, in Spitalfields.

Leman trained as a designer as well as a manufacturer, very unusually for the English industry. Smith's *Laboratory or School of Arts* (1756 edition) records that every Lyon manufacturer was a pattern drawer but 'On the contrary here in England, take London and Canterbury together, I know of no more than one manufacturer thus qualified, as was the late ingenious Mr Lemon in his time'. The museum's earliest designs by him are dated 1706, just four years from the start of his apprenticeship, some inscribed 'For my father, Peter Leman, by me, James Leman'. In 1711 he was admitted as 'For[eign] Master' to the Weavers' Company, and on his father's death in 1712 he took over the family business.

As well as producing his own accomplished silk designs Leman engaged other designers to supply him, including Christopher Baudouin and Joseph Dandridge, both well known in their day. The latest designs known to be by Leman are dated 1722, but there is no reason to believe he gave up this side of his profession after that time. Part of the canopy used at George II's Coronation in 1727, now in the V&A's collection, was supplied by the mercer

George Binckes, known to have bought designs from Leman: it is very similar in style to his work and may well have been designed by him.

Leman rose to high office in the Weavers' Company, becoming a Liveryman and member of the Court of Assistants; in 1731 he was elected Renter Bailiff, second-in-command in the Company. He was clearly an energetic and capable man, actively involved on a number of Committees working for Weavers' Company interests, and in the year of his death, 1745, he helped organize the campaign being launched against the sellers and wearers of printed calico.

James Leman was talented in a number of fields, and the diversity of his interests is revealed by his will : 'my paintings, drawings and all my collection of prints, my reading books, my musick and picture books and my collection of copy books, my musical and my mathematical instruments of all sorts, my collection of reptiles in spirits, my collection of medals and coins, with several odd things', all to be distributed by his wife to his surviving children.

Christopher Baudouin

Christopher Baudouin was described in Smith's *Laboratory or School of Arts* (1756 edition) as 'the first that brought the flower'd silk manufacture in credit and reputation here in England'. He was a Huguenot refugee, possibly from Tours, and was active in London from the 1680s, being naturalized with his wife and daughters in 1709, and signing himself, in a petition in 1714, as one of 'the Gentleman and Principal Inhabitants of the Hamlet of Spitalfields'. His earliest extant design, dated 1707, was to be woven by the Lemans for Matthew Vernon, a mercer with a royal appointment, and Baudouin was still producing work for James Leman in 1718, while his designs produced in the later 1720s, delicate, accomplished and still highly fashionable, were collected by Garthwaite among her 'Patterns by Different Hands'. He had died some time before 1736, when his widow drew up her own will.

Joseph Dandridge

A silk designer by profession, Joseph Dandridge was also a distinguished botanist, entomologist and ornithologist, described by a former pupil as 'a person of unbounded curiosity and unwearied application in his researches into the works of nature'. He was born in Buckinghamshire in 1665, the son of a barber-surgeon, and came to London as an apprentice in 1679. The extant silk designs that can be attributed to him, commissioned by James Leman, date from between 1717 and 1722, but Malachy Postlethwayt in *The Universal Dictionary of Trade and Commerce* (1757) described him as a silk designer for 'near forty years'. He was said to have been particularly good at designing damasks, while the patterns he prepared for Leman were for the richest silks, to be executed chiefly in gold and silver thread. He may have continued as a silk designer into the 1730s, when he had as his pupil John Vansommer, who would become a distinguished designer in his turn. Dandridge died in 1746.

Bibliography

D.E. Allen, 'Joseph Dandridge and the first
  Aurelian Society', *Entomologists' Record*,
  vol. 78 (1966)

W.S. Bristow, 'The Life and Work of a Great
  English Naturalist Joseph Dandridge
  1664–1746', *Entomologists' Gazette*,
  vol. 18 (1967)

Savary de Bruslons, *Dictionnaire Universel de
  Commerce*, Paris 1723

Anne Buck, *Dress in Eighteenth-century
  England*, London 1979

J. Southerden Burn, *The History of the French,
  Walloon, Dutch, and other Foreign
  Protestant Refugees settled in England*,
  London 1846

D.C. Coleman, *Courtaulds: an economic and
  social history*, 2 vols, Oxford 1969

Ulla Cyrus-Zetterstrom, *Handbok i Vavning*,
  American edition 1956

Mrs Delany, *The Autobiography and
  Correspondence of Mary Granville,
  Mrs Delany: with interesting reminiscences
  of King George the Third and Queen
  Charlotte*, ed. the Rt. Hon. Lady Llanover,
  London 1861

Diderot, *Encyclopédie*, Paris 1754

An Elegant Art, exhibition catalogue ed.
  Edward Maeder, Los Angeles County
  Museum of Art 1983

Gentleman's Magazine, 1731 onwards

J. Godart, *L'Ouvrier en Soie*, Lyon 1899

John Gwynn, *An Essay on Design*, London 1749

E. Hidemark (ed.), *18th-Century Textiles,
  The Anders Berch Collection at the Nordiska
  Museet*, Stockholm 1990

Luther Hooper, *Hand-loom Weaving, Plain &
  Ornamental*, London 1910

*House of Commons Journals, Select Committee
  Reports*, especially vol. 30 pp. 208–19 March
  1765 and pp. 724–29 April 1766

Joubert de L'Hiberderie, *Le dessinateur pour
  les fabriques d'étoffes d'or, d'argent et de
  soie*, Paris 1765

Donald King (ed.), *British Textile Design in the
  Victoria and Albert Museum*, vols I and II,
  Gakken, Tokyo 1980 (reissued as *The
  Victoria and Albert Museum's Textile
  Collection*, see Rothstein, Natalie)

'Spitalfields and Mile End New Town'. Walter Ison and P.A. Bezodis (eds). *London County Council Survey of London*. vol. XXVII. London 1957

W. and S. Minet (eds). *Livre des Temoignages de l'Eglise de Threadneedle Street, 1669–1789*. London 1909

Florence Montgomery. *Textiles in America 1650–1870*. New York and London 1984

John Murphy. *A Treatise on the Art of Weavig*. Glasgow 1827

J. Paulet. *L'art du fabriquant d'étoffes de soies*. Paris 1789

Norma Perry. 'John Vansommer of Spitalfields. Huguenot, silk designer and correspondent of Voltaire', in *Studies on Voltaire and the 18th Century*. LX. Institut et Musée Voltaire. Les Delices. Geneva 1968

Malachy Postlethwayt. *The Universal Dictionary of Trade and Commerce*. London 1751

The Quiet Conquest: the Huguenots 1685–1985. exhibition catalogue. Museum of London 1985

Registers of the French Church at Threadneedle Street. pub. The Huguenot Society. London. and other publications by the Society

Aileen Ribeiro. *Dress in Eighteenth-Century Europe 1715–1789*. London 1984

Rococo, Art and Design in Hogarth's England. exhibition catalogue. V&A 1984

Natalie Rothstein. 'The Silk Industry in London 1702–66'. London MA thesis 1961

— 'The Calico Campaign of 1719–21', *East London Papers*. vol. 7. no. 1 (July 1964)

— 'Dutch Silks – An important but forgotten industry of the 18th century or a hypothesis?', *Oud Holland*. no. 3 (1964)

— 'Joseph Dandridge, Naturalist and Silk Designer'. *East London Papers*. vol. 9. no. 2 (1966). pp. 101–18

— 'Silks for the American Market', *Connoisseur*. vol. 166, nos 168, 169 (October and November 1967)

— 'The introduction of the jacquard loom to Great Britain', in *Studies in Textile History*. ed. Veronika Gervers. Toronto 1977

— 'Les Protestants Normands dans la Soierie Londonienne'. *Minorités religieuses en Normandie*. Actes du XXe Congrès de la Société Historique et Archéologique de Normandie. Rouen 1985

— (ed.) *Barbara Johnson's Album of Fashions and Fabrics*. London and New York 1987

— 'Canterbury and London. the silk industry in the late 17th century'. *Textile History*. vol. 20. no. 1 (1989)

— 'L'organisation du commerce des soieries en France et en Angleterre au XVIIIe siècle'. *Le Monde alpin et rhodanien*. 2e–3e trimestres 1991. pp. 85–92

— 'The successful and the unsuccessful Huguenot. another look at the London silk industry in the 18th and early 19th centuries'. *Proceedings of the Huguenot Society* XXV (5) 1993. pp. 439–50

— 'Fashion. silk and the Worshipful Company of Weavers' in *La Seta in Europa Secc. XIII–XX*. Istituto Internationale di Storia Economica Datini. Prato. 1993. pp. 465–85

— *The Victoria and Albert Museum's Textile Collection: Woven Textile Design in Britain to 1750*. London 1994 (part reissue of D. King (ed.). *British Textile Design in the Victoria and Albert Museum*. vol I. 1980)

— *The Victoria and Albert Museum's Textile Collection: Woven Textile Design in Britain from 1750 to 1850*. London 1994 (part reissue of D. King (ed.). *British Textile Design in the Victoria and Albert Museum*. vol II. 1980)

Rouquet. *L'Etat des Arts en Angleterre*. Paris 1755

I. Scouloudi (ed.). *Huguenots in Britain and their French Background, 1550–1800*. London 1987

G. Smith. *Laboratory or School of Arts*. London 1756 edition

Peter K. Thornton. 'An 18th-Century Silk Designer's Manual'. *Bulletin of the Needle and Bobbin Club, New York*. vol. 42. nos 1 and 2 (1958)

— 'Jean Revel. Dessinateur de la Grande Fabrique'. *Gazette des Beaux Arts*. vol. LVI (1960)

— *Baroque and Rococo Silks*. London 1965

Peter K. Thornton and N. Rothstein. 'The Importance of the Huguenots in the London Silk Industry'. *Proceedings of the History Society of London*. vol. XX. no. 1 (1959)

Worshipful Company of Weavers, Court Books (Guildhall Library MSS department)

Index of Colour Plates

Dimensions are first given in inches, with centimetres in parentheses

plate	museum no.	plate	museum no.	plate	museum no.
1	E.1861.35–1991	41	E.4446–1909	81	5974.4
2	E.1861.15–1991	42	5970.1	82	E.1861.2–1991
3	E.1861.6–1991	43	5970.21	83	5971.24
4	E.1861.34–1991	44	5970.9A	84	5974.2A
5	E.1861.57–1991	45	5971.5	85	5974.30
6	E.1861.41–1991	46	5970.18	86	5974.23
7	E.1861.67–1991	47	5970.11	87	5974.27
8	T. 221–1987	48	5970.26	88	5974.25
9	E.1861.52–1991	49	5970.43	89	5974.21
10	E.1861.66–1991	50	5971.4	90	5974.29
11	E.1861.102–1991	51	5970.8A	91	5974.22
12	E.1861.95–1991	52	5975.8	92	5974.22
13	E.1861.98–1991	53	5975.11	93	5974.26
14	E.1861.72–1991	54	5975.10	94	5974.15
15	E.1861.73–1991	55	5971.6	95	5974.13
16	E.1861.80–1991	56	5971.6	96	5978.10
17	E.1861.88–1991	57	T.837–1974	97	5978.5
18	E.1861.31–1991	58	5975.16	98	5978.14
19	E.1861.28–1991	59	5971.13	99	5981.8A
20	E.1861.89–1991	60	5975.17	100	5979.4
21	E.1861.58–1991	61	5971.11	101	5979.14
22	E.1861.27–1991	62	5974.5	102	5977.13
23	E.1861.27–1991	63	5974.5	103	5977.14
24	E.1861.22–1991	64	5975.13	104	5977.21
25	E.1861.32–1991	65	5977.24A	105	5979.18
26	E.1861.38–1991	66	5974.10	106	5971.29
27	E.1861.26–1991	67	5972.16	107	5980.5
28	E.1861.37–1991	68	5973.23	108	5980.5
29	E.4481–1909	69	5972.13	109	5981.4A
30	E.1861.4–1991	70	5977.23A&B	110	5980.14
31	E.4440–1909	71	5977.11	111	5979.5
32	E.4451–1909	72	5977.10	112	5981.6A
33	E.4465–1909	73	5974.1.	113	5981.9&9A
34	E.4469–1909	74	E.1861.85–1991	114	5980.12
35	E.4472–1909	75	5974.2	115	5981.20
36	E.4511–1909	76	5977.24	116	5980.9
37	5973.22	77	5974.6	117	5981.10B
38	E.4502–1909	78	5972.26	118	5981.1A
39	E.4502–1909	79	5972.22	119	5981.5
40	5973.17	80	5974.3	120	5981.15A

plate	museum no.		plate	museum no.		plate	museum no.
121	5980.15		161	5986.12		188	T.406–1972
122	5980.15		162	5988.9[IV]		189	T.421–1972
123	5980.15		163	5989.9		190	T.374–1972 p. 94
124	5981.22A		164	5988.13			3¼ × 9 (8.3 × 22.9)
125	5981.12A&B		165	5989.1		191	T.374–1972 p. 221
126	5981.22A		166	5989.22			6¾ × 10 (17.2 × 25.4)
127	5981.12		167	5990.17		192	T.373–1972 p. 37V.
128	5981.2A		168	5990.16			lower 8 × 21¾
129	5981.2A		169	T.375–1972 p. 28			(20.3 × 55.3)
130	T.392–1971 p. 27			3¾ × 10½ (9.5 × 26.7)			English samples
131	T.392–1971 p. 3		170	T.375–1972 p. 239			inserted later.
132	T.391–1971 p. 85			3½ × 10⅜ (8.9 × 26.4)			one from T.374–1972
133	T.392–1971 p. 50		171	T.375–1972 p. 74		193	T.374–1972 p. 121
134	T.391–1971 p. 109			3 × 10 (7.6 × 25.4)			5 × 9½ (12.7 × 24.1)
135	T.392–1971 p. 77		172	T.375–1972 p. 121		194	T.374–1972 p. 53
136	T.392–1971 p. 49			4½ × 10 (11.4 × 25.4)			8¼ × 5¼ (20.9 × 13.3)
137	T.391–1971 p. 75		173	T.373–1972 p. 67V		195	T.374–1972 p. 74
138	T.393–1971 p. 1			11 × 21½ (27.9 × 54.6)			1½ × 7½ (3.8 × 19.1)
139	T.392–1971 p. 93		174	T.373–1972 p. 52		196	T.374–1972 p. 68
140	T.391–1971 p. 9			11½ × 21¾ (29.2 × 55.3)			1¾ × 11¾ (4.5 × 29.9)
141	T.391–1971 p. 9		175	T.375–1972 p. 306		197	T.374–1972 p. 27
142	T.392–1971 p. 61			2½ × 10¾ (6.4 × 27.3)			upper 2½ × 10½
143	T.391–1971 p. 97		176	T.375–1972 p. 270			(6.4 × 26.7)
144	T.392–1971 p. 61			5¾ × 6½ (14.6 × 16.5)		198	T.374–1972 p. 27
145	T.391–1971 p. 97		177	T.375–1972 p. 279			upper 2½ × 10½
146	T.393–1971 p. 9			6¼ × 9½ (15.9 × 24.1)			(6.4 × 26.7)
147	T.393–1971 p. 21		178	T.373–1972 p. 7V		199	T.374–1972 p. 13
148	5982.21			9½ × 14 (24.1 × 35.6)			2½ × 11 (6.4 × 27.9)
149	5984.17		179	T.373–1972 p. 48		200	T.374–1972 p. 13
150	T.392–1988			14 × 20 (35.6 × 50.8)			2½ × 11 (6.4 × 27.9)
151	5983.8		180	T.375–1972 p. 125		201	T.374–1972 p. 292
152	5983.7			6 × 2½ (15.2 × 6.4)			2 × 10 (5.1 × 25.4)
153	5984.14		181	T.375–1972 p. 125		202	T.377–1972 p. 63
154	5984.15			6 × 2½ (15.2 × 6.4)			upper colourway 1⅞ × 6¼
155	5985.13		182	T.408–1972			(4.8 × 15.9)
156	5986.9		183	T.413–1972		203	T.374–1972 p. 296
157	5985.10		184	T.409–1972			2½ × 11 (6.4 × 27.9)
158	5985.38		185	T.423–1972		204	T.377–1972 p. 69
159	5985.31		186	T.404–1972			upper colourway 2½ × 11¾
160	5985.36		187	T.417–1972			(6.4 × 29.9)

plate	*museum no.*	*plate*	*museum no.*	*plate*	*museum no.*
205	T.380–1972 p. 24	223	T.384–1972 p. 262.	242	T.376–1972 p. 147)
	6 × 10½ (15.2 × 26.7)		3⅜ × 9⅝ (8.6 × 24.5)		4¼ × 10½ (10.8 × 26.7)
206	T.376–1972 p. 33	224	T.384–1972 p. 186	243	T.382–1972 p. 177
	9½ × 7 (24.1 × 17.8)		6 × 9¼ (15.2 × 23.5)		3 × 12½ (7.6 × 31.8)
207	T.377–1972 p. 130	225	T.384–1972 p. 151	244	T.382–1972 p. 177
	colourway 2¼ × 7⅜		2⅝ × 9 (6.7 × 22.9)		3 × 12½ (7.6 × 31.8)
	(5.7 × 18.7)	226	T.371–1972	245	T.382–1972 p. 156
208	T.380–1972 p. 14	227	T.384–1972 p. 177		3 × 6¼ (7.6 × 15.9)
	1¼ × 1 (3.2 × 2.5)		5¼ × 9 (13.3 × 22.9)	246	T.382–1972 p. 280
209	T.384–1972 p. 81	228	T.378–1972 p. 259		3 × 12½ (7.6 × 31.8)
	3⅝ × 9½ (9.2 × 24.1)		11 × 2¾ (27.9 × 6.9)	247	T.379–1972 p. 42
210	T.377–1972 p. 168	229	T.378–1972 p. 317		10 × 4 (25.4 × 10.2)
	colourway 1½ × 6		left 10 × 6¼	248	T.379–1972 p. 145
	(3.8 × 15.2)		(25.4 × 15.9)		5¼ × 9½ (13.3 × 24.1)
211	T.378–1972 p. 63	230	T.378–1972 p. 243	249	T.379–1972 p. 85
	2¼ × 8¾ (5.7 × 22.2)		5¼ × 1 (14.6 × 2.5)		18 × 9½ (45.7 × 24.1)
212	T.377–1972 p. 314	231	T.378–1972 p. 240	250	T.379–1972 p. 122
	3½ × 7 (8.9 × 17.8)		3¾ × 10 (9.5 × 25.4)		upper 4 × 10 (10.2 × 25.4)
213	T.378–1972 p. 161	232	T.89–1973 p. 15	251	T.379–1972 p. 323
	upper 3 × 6¼ (7.6 × 15.9)		3¼ × 12 (8.3 × 30.5)		3½ × 5½ (8.9 × 13.9)
214	T.376–1972 p. 78	233	T.89–1973 p. 67	252	T.385–1972 p. 6
	colourway 3¼ × 8		11½ × 12 (29.2 × 30.5)		colourway 2 × 3¾
	(8.3 × 20.3)	234	T.378–1972 p. 345		(5.1 × 9.5)
215	T.384–1972 p. 225		7 × 11 (17.8 × 27.9)	253	T.385–1972 p. 116
	4⅜ × 9½ (11.1 × 24.1)	235	T.89–1973 p. 105		colourway 2 × 4
216	T.89–1924		10¼ × 11¼ (26 × 28.6)		(5.1 × 10.2)
	Can be identified	236	T.89–1973 p. 138	254	T.385–1972 p. 19
	from T.384–1972 p. 225		2¾ × 5½ (6.9 × 13.9)		10 × 21½ (25.4 × 54.6)
217	T.384–1972 p. 37	237	T.376–1972 p. 139	255	T.385–1972 p. 271
	3¾ × 10 (9.5 × 25.4)		right 4 × 20½		colourway 2½ × 10
218	T.384–1972 p. 121		(10.2 × 52.1)		(5.7 × 25.4)
	3⅛ × 6 (7.9 × 15.2)	238	T.89–1973 p. 148	256	T.385–1972 p. 271
219	T.384–1972 p. 87		2½ × 12 (6.4 × 30.5)		colourway 2½ × 10
	4½ × 9⅜ (11.4 × 23.8)	239	T.376–1972 p. 128		(5.7 × 25.4)
220	T.384–1972 p. 234		2¾ × 9¾ (6.9 × 24.8)	257	T.385–1972 p. 172
	6½ × 8¾ (15.2 × 22.2)	240	T.382–1972 p. 47		3 × 3½ (7.6 × 8.9)
221	T.384–1972 p. 126		2⅜ × 11¾ (6 × 29.9)	258	T.383–1972
	2⅞ × 6 (7.3 × 15.2)	241	T.378–1972 p. 360		2 × 3¾ (5.1 × 9.5)
222	T.384–1972 p. 96.		centre 2 × 2½	259	T.383–1972
	3⅝ × 9¼ (9.2 × 23.5)		(5.1 × 6.4)		1¾ × 4⅜ (4.5 × 11.1)